Put Beginning Readers on the Right Track with
ALL ABOARD READING™

The All Aboard Reading series is especially designed for beginning readers. Written by noted authors and illustrated in full color, these are books that children really want to read—books to excite their imagination, expand their interests, make them laugh, and support their feelings. With fiction and non-fiction stories that are high interest and curriculum-related, All Aboard Reading books offer something for every young reader. And with four different reading levels, the All Aboard Reading series lets you choose which books are most appropriate for your children and their growing abilities.

Picture Readers
Picture Readers have super-simple texts, with many nouns appearing as rebus pictures. At the end of each book are 24 flash cards—on one side is a rebus picture; on the other side is the written-out word.

Station Stop 1
Station Stop 1 books are best for children who have just begun to read. Simple words and big type make these early reading experiences more comfortable. Picture clues help children to figure out the words on the page. Lots of repetition throughout the text helps children to predict the next word or phrase—an essential step in developing word recognition.

Station Stop 2
Station Stop 2 books are written specifically for children who are reading with help. Short sentences make it easier for early readers to understand what they are reading. Simple plots and simple dialogue help children with reading comprehension.

Station Stop 3
Station Stop 3 books are perfect for children who are reading alone. With longer text and harder words, these books appeal to children who have mastered basic reading skills. More complex stories captivate children who are ready for more challenging books.

In addition to All Aboard Reading books, look for All Aboard Math Readers™ (fiction stories that teach math concepts children are learning in school) and All Aboard Science Readers™ (nonfiction books that explore the most fascinating science topics in age-appropriate language).

All Aboard for happy reading!

For Craig, Drew, Josh, Chris, Patt, and Dean.
My brother, brothers-in-law, and brothers in
life, who give men a good name—G.C.

For Kathy, Stephanie and Christopher who
always give support and inspiration—S.J.P.

Text copyright © 2001 by Ginjer Clarke. Illustrations copyright © 2001 by Steven James
Petruccio. All rights reserved. Published by Grosset & Dunlap, a division of Penguin Putnam
Books for Young Readers, 345 Hudson Street, New York, NY 10014. ALL ABOARD SCIENCE
READER and GROSSET & DUNLAP are trademarks of Penguin Putnam Inc. Published
simultaneously in Canada. Printed in the U.S.A.

Library of Congress Catalog Card Number: 2002275378

ISBN 0-488-42490-8   N O P Q R S T

SHARKS!

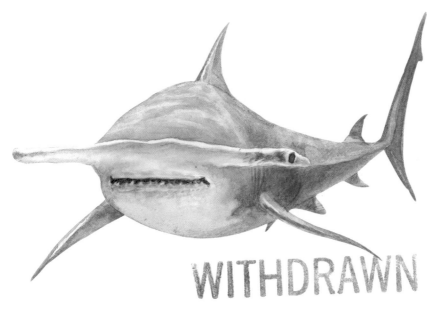

WITHDRAWN

By Ginjer Clarke

Illustrated by Steven James Petruccio

Grosset & Dunlap • New York

Hawaii

It is a hot day.
A surfer waits
for a big wave.

All at once,
something bumps
his board!

Then he sees a fin.

It is a shark!

The surfer swims away.

He is safe.
But he needs
a new board!

Sharks do not bite
people very often.
Surfers look like seals
to hungry sharks.
And sharks love to eat seals.

The most dangerous shark
is the great white shark.

It has a white belly.

It is very big.

Great white sharks eat seals,
fish,
turtles,
penguins,
and even other sharks.

The great white has
many rows of teeth.
Sometimes a tooth breaks.
Then a tooth from behind
takes its place.

Are all sharks dangerous?
No!
The biggest shark
is the whale shark.
It is longer than
a school bus.

The whale shark
eats only tiny fish and shrimp.
It will let a diver
go for a ride on its fins.

basking shark

These sharks
are also very big.

megamouth shark

They do not bite people.
All they eat are
tiny shrimp and animals.

17

Are all sharks big?

No.

Lots of sharks are small.
This shark is only
as big as a cat.
But it has sharp teeth!

cookie cutter shark

The smallest shark
is about as long as a pencil.
It lives at the bottom
of the sea.
Its eyes glow.
It can see in the dark water!

lantern shark

lemon shark

blue shark

pink goblin shark

There are about
375 kinds of sharks.
They come in many
colors and shapes.

leopard shark

This shark
has spots.

This shark has eyes
on the ends
of its head.

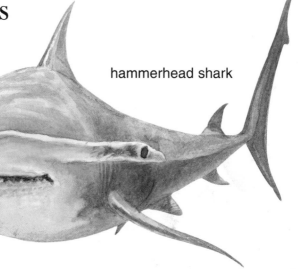

hammerhead shark

This shark's head is
shaped like a saw.

saw shark

This shark
is the color of sand.
It is hard to see
on the floor of the sea.
There is fringe
all around its mouth.

wobbegong shark

The fringe looks
like seaweed.
Fish do not see its teeth—
until it is too late!

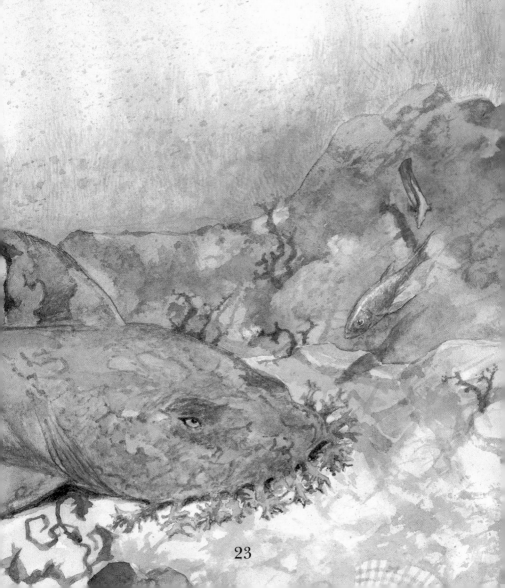

All sharks are fish.

But they do not have bones.

Their skeleton and jaws
are made of cartilage.

(You say it like
this: car-till-lej.)

Cartilage is strong.

But it bends.

Your ears
and nose
are made
of cartilage.

Like all fish,
sharks have gills.
They breathe water
through their gills.

Like all fish,
some sharks lay eggs.
Shark eggs look
like small purses.
The baby sharks
hatch from the egg cases.

But most sharks
give birth to baby sharks.
Baby sharks are called pups.

Great white pups
are as big as you are.

The mother shark
does not take care
of the baby sharks.
Right away the pups
start hunting.
They are on their own.

Sharks have been around
for a long, long time.
Before dinosaurs,
there were sharks.

Sharks will be around
for a long time
to come.

A COUNSELOR CAN HELP

We HAVE STRESSED the need for facing our grief, and for talking out our emotional tensions. The question then arises: To whom shall we talk? Often we can talk to relatives or friends who have proper sympathy and a willingness to listen. There are times when bereaved persons can talk out their grief together. But often others do not make good listeners, or there are concerns that we do not wish to express to them. Other members of our immediate family may have such a strong need to express themselves that we cannot expect them to listen to us. Well-meaning friends often block our show of emotion with advice to brace up, and to keep a calm appearance. Frequently they try to change the subject to something more pleasant or less personal. Or perhaps they find some excuse to leave, because they are disturbed themselves over an emotional situation that they feel inadequate to handle. Many of the things that we want to say may be intimate and personal, so that we do not want them to become neighborhood gossip. Some concerns may reflect on ourselves, or at least we fear others might think so, and thus we do not want to express our innermost feelings to someone who might condemn us. For one of several different reasons others may not qualify as persons to whom we are willing to express our strongest feelings. To whom, then, shall we go? Possibly to more than one. Maybe not.

The first one to be contacted will likely be our minister. If there has been a protracted illness, he will undoubtedly be in close contact with us anyway. If it is apparent that the end is imminent, we shall want to call him to be there when the blow falls. If the end comes unexpectedly or at an uncertain hour, we shall want to call him as soon as we realize what has happened. He should be called as soon, at least, as we call the funeral director. It is not true consideration to wait until a convenient hour to notify him. He will want to be of service, and during those first hours of shock he can at least stand by as one who cares. Maybe the numbness will be so great that we shall not want to talk, or possibly the fact of what has occurred will not have been fully realized as yet. It isn't necessary at this early hour to force oneself to talk in a way in which we are not ready to talk. It is enough that the minister is there, and that his presence speaks of his concern. He can be a strength that others might not be because he has had more experience with death than most of us. He has stood in the presence of death many times before, and so is not so overawed by it as those who may be facing it for the first time. Furthermore, while he is deeply concerned, he is not so emotionally involved as we whose beloved has died. Let us call our minister immediately when death comes to our loved ones.

After the funeral, instead of having the counselor come to us, it is better for us to go to him. In a controlled situation, e.g., in the minister's study, free from interruptions from the family, we can talk. This counseling should begin within a very few days of the funeral. The sooner it is started, the less time it will take to free ourselves from grief and its accompanying emotions such as guilt. The longer our emotions have had a hold upon us, the longer it will take to break their destructive power over us. If we start counseling right away after the funeral, and talk for approximately an hour once or twice a week, the sharp edge of our grief should be dissolved in from six to ten weeks. In severe grief, pain will come back with memories for many months, but the destructive force will be gone. The length of an interview may vary a little from an hour, but not much. Much less than an hour doesn't allow time enough for full release of feelings, while much over an hour becomes tiring to both ourselves and the counselor. Seldom is much release achieved in a longer period.

The counselor to whom we go may be our minister, a physician, or a wise friend. We should choose him carefully. He should be one who by training and temperament is qualified to be a good counselor. Not all ministers have these qualifications. The average person doesn't. However, if we give a little consideration to our quest, we can find someone who has the ability, the inclination, and the time to help us.

A good counselor will be one who is not himself undergoing a grief experience or some other emotional upset. He must be emotionally mature. He will need to have patience and to be disciplined so that he will allow us to talk about anything we wish to discuss. Too many people will be ready with quick advice, or will want to tell of some experience of their own or of some situation about which they have heard. This will break our trend of thought, prevent us from getting the emotional release we need, and soon discourage us from trying to get help. If our counselor proves to have these failings, then we should seek another one at once.

Not only is a good counselor willing to listen, but he can't be shocked. We don't need to be afraid to unburden our most trying concerns in a direct and straightforward manner. His purpose is not to judge us, but to help us, and to this end he will accept us as we are without alarm. Furthermore, he has experienced enough of life to know what is in man, and to know that even saints have thoughts and desires that are not always conventional or socially approved. He knows that the best of people have said and done things that they would not want generally known. He knows, furthermore, that one who has unconventional thoughts or desires, or has done things that he ought not to have done, is not thereby depraved or inherently bad. Such a person needs help in becoming the person he would like to be, and a good counselor is ready and willing to give that help.

Another point to consider in choosing our counselor is that a good one will not betray confidences. One who is given to passing on to others the things that people tell him is not one to whom we want to tell our inmost thoughts. A good counselor will not, under any pretense, or under however veiled a manner, use confidences as a subject of discussion with anyone. To prying neighbors or acquaintances he gives no satisfaction, not the slightest clue or intimation that he has heard anything not already generally known. A good counselor doesn't forget. Our problems remain as a burden and a concern on his heart. But they are securely locked from prying eyes and public exposure. Unless we confide to others also, our secrets remain in the closed triangle of ourselves, our counselor, and God.

Yet another point to consider in choosing our counselor is that we seek one who is not himself emotionally involved with us or our problem. When we have fallen into a stream and are in need of assistance, we can get much more help from one whose feet are firmly planted on the bank than we can from one who has fallen in with us, and is himself in need of assistance. One who is too much involved emotionally in us or our plight will not be a firm enough anchor to which to tie. A good counselor has concern, to be sure, but he also has a certain separateness from us and our problem. Just as surgeons do not operate on members of their own immediate families, so a good counselor for us in grief is one whose affections are not involved.

Yet a further quality to look for in our counselor is that he have faith — faith in life, faith in us, and faith in God. One who is cynical or fearful or defeated in life won't be able to inspire us to have courage and confidence. To help us, he must have faith in the basic soundness and creativeness of life itself. If he does not believe that life has meaning, he will not be the sound anchorage that we need in our time of turmoil.

There should be faith in us in particular. Unless he believes that we have a basic soundness in our personality that will enable us to overcome our present handicaps, he is not likely to inspire that belief in us. Unless he believes that in us are the basic forces for creative growth, he will seldom lead us in that larger experience that makes for emotional health. Usually we shall know enough about our counselor before we go to him to decide whether he has this quality or not. If we find that the one to whom we have gone falls short, then the sooner we seek another the better.

Having chosen our counselor, what can we expect to get from the counseling situation? Several results should be forthcoming, the most immediate of which is emotional support. The counselor will partially fill the terrible emptiness which is left when our loved one dies. This isn't solely a matter of physical presence. It is a common experience that a person can be most lonely in the very midst of a crowd. The hurrying, impersonal mob in the congested city can push and shove us around, but leave us alone and isolated. To be company, there must be bonds of common concern. This others may not provide. Other members of the family are likely to be primarily concerned with the way the loss affects them. Friends and neighbors may have been helpful between the time of death and the burial, but once the funeral is over, we are left very much alone. Other people may be present with us most of the time, but they may have no feeling for our problem, or no realization that it is there. They don't mean to be indifferent, but our ache is down deep inside and doesn't show. For them, the death of our beloved may be an event that has been pushed into the background by the pressure of daily activities. For us it remains an inward pain of loneliness.

Our counselor will help to overcome our loneliness and to ease the pain. For one hour at least his primary concern is the need we have for overcoming our grief. He wants to share the burdens of our hearts. No matter what other interests are crowding in for his attention, they are pushed back of the limits set for our visit. Now his whole attention is reserved for us. We can talk and know that he is listening, not only with his ears, but with his heart as well. The emptiness of our lives is filled temporarily, in part at least, by one who is interested. The loneliness is overcome by one who shares our concerns. The burden of our grief grows lighter because here is one who shares it with us.

The second thing that we can expect to get from our visits with a counselor is release from our emotional tensions. Our feelings of loss and sorrow, of appreciation, of hostility, and of guilt, all mingle to create this tension, and all must be talked out if the tension is to be released. We can talk to our counselor in the full assurance that if the pain of our memories becomes overwhelming, and we break down in a period of sobbing, that is all right too. That too is release, and a wise counselor will not try to stop us. Neither will he be embarrassed or impatient with us. He will be sympathetic, sitting quietly by and waiting for us to take up our story in any way we desire.

When we talk to the counselor, we are not talking to give him information. Considerable information will be involved, of course, but that is a secondary consideration. We have noted in choosing our counselor that he was one who would keep our confidences, so that is no worry. On the other hand, there is no need to try to give a consecutive or consistent story. We can let our thoughts roam where they will and talk of things as they occur to us. In the midst of telling of a recent incident our thoughts may jump back over the years to something that we hadn't thought of for a long time. Let them go. Telling of this may have a far more helpful effect upon us than finishing the story we first started, and the fact that the counselor doesn't get a complete story doesn't count at all.

The thing that is distressing to us sometimes, and often prevents us from getting the emotional release we should, is that when we allow our thoughts to wander, we tell a contradictory story. But that isn't important, either. The primary purpose of our visit with the counselor is to get release from our tensions. These may be especially strong because we do have contradictory feelings. If in the midst of our expression of appreciation, some angry thought breaks in, let us not try to suppress it. The counselor will understand, and we shall be better off for having it out. Eventually, as we continue to talk, these memories will all lose their emotional charge, and we shall be able to handle them without undue pain.

Along with the loss of emotional tension will come the development of insight and understanding. As we talk, our own thoughts will become clearer. We shall see our situation more objectively. We shall understand better the feelings that have disturbed us in the past, and why we have felt as we have in our bereavement. One man said that he thought with his pencil. Most of us think better, and can get a clearer picture of what we ourselves believe or want to do about a specific situation, when we have an opportunity to talk through the various possibilities with someone else. As we talk to our counselor about the pain of loneliness that is in us, we come to see more clearly what troubles us, and what we can do about it.

As we talk we shall get a clearer evaluation of the deceased.

During our lives together we were too closely wrapped up in our immediate relationships to be completely objective in our judgments. We had been so busy living together that we hadn't stood apart to evaluate our beloved. Alternate emotions of love and anger had caused us, probably, to be first too romantic in our evaluation and then too harsh. Now that the relationship is broken, there is an opportunity to stand aside, to review it completely, and to evaluate it more accurately. In the permissive relationship that we have with the counselor, we are enabled for the first time, perhaps, really to understand our beloved. Here for the first time, too, we gain an insight into our own feelings for him, and see more clearly not only how we felt toward him, but why we felt as we did.

As we talk to the counselor, we gain further insight into our present grief feelings. We see them as the pain of our own loneliness. Once we understand this, we can do something about it. While we can't bring back our beloved, we can take steps to overcome the pain that his going caused. This event can be evaluated in the total picture of our lives so that our loss doesn't eclipse everything else. We see not only what is gone, but also what is left. Readjustment to the world from which our beloved is gone becomes possible.

RELIGION HELPS

HAVING SEEN what grief is, and noted what we ought to do about it, the time has come to consider the help our religion has for us. Let us be cautioned again, however, that religion is not a substitute for grief, nor an instrument of suppression. It is a power which will help us to meet grief head on, to pass through it, and to come out on the other side strengthened by the experience.

At the foundation of our religious strength is our belief in God. This means that the ultimate reality in the universe is a divine Person. At the heart of the universe is a dynamic self-conscious Being with whom men can have a deeper fellowship. We have not come to this planet accidentally, nor been put here by an arbitrary fate. Neither were our ancestors put here long ago, and then left to themselves alone. Our belief is in a living God, infinitely great, but also dynamically immediate and near. He is constantly at work at the unfinished business of creation, not only in the larger universe around us, but in the intimate personal world within each of us. The depths of our inner persons have communion with the depths of the Person everywhere present, who at the same time is adequate to our needs for understanding and strength.

This implies the worth of every individual. Death may come and sweep away a meaningful companionship, with apparent disregard for us and our beloved. Our Christian faith, however, assures us that this is not the caprice of a fate that utterly disregards us and our feelings. Each of us is loved by God as one of his creatures, and our heartaches are a part of the heartache of God who expressed his love in the cross of Christ. This worth, furthermore, is not dependent on outward circumstances, but is an intrinsic value which each of us possesses by virtue of his humanity. Once again, this value persists in spite of our failures and our sins. It is an intrinsic value derived from our creation by our Heavenly Father. At the heart of the universe, and at the very foundation of our own lives, is our God.

Our belief in God implies, further, the embodiment of divine purpose in the universe. At times we have felt bewildered by what seemed to be the caprices of nature in storm and disaster. Again we have been overwhelmed by the impartiality in the operation of its laws without regard for human interests or life. Our faith assures us, however, that although the ultimate purpose is not readily ascertainable in certain specific happenings, yet it is there. Death disrupts men's plans and breaks up their cherished fellowships in what seems at times to be a cruel disregard for their welfare and desires. The particular death that took our loved one may seem to us to be especially callous. Yet our Christian faith enables us to see this in terms of a larger setting which in the long run adds up to a creative pattern in the eternal purpose of God.

Another way of clarifying this point is to see it in terms of the ultimate triumph of good over evil. Life holds so many experiences that are harsh and cruel and appear to go without compensation that one looking at the contemporary scene might be overcome with despair. Our confidence is in God, however, and in both his desire to bring things out and his ability so to do. In the long run the events that appear to be so overwhelmingly evil will be dissolved in the beneficent purpose of God.

In the case of death this is summed up in the doctrine of the resurrection. Stated in various ways, this doctrine adds up to the belief that death is not the end, but is rather a transition to another room in our Father's house. The loved one is not gone, but gone before, and in a later life we shall meet him, and know him, and have fellowship with him again. Death of our loved one may be all loss for us at the time, but it is all gain for our beloved, and in the long run of eternity it will be all gain for us too. An acceptance of this doctrine helps us to evaluate our grief correctly. We see clearly now that our pain is for our own loneliness, and that it is on this basis that we shall have to work it out. This is not to minimize our pain, but it is to understand it. This doesn't take our pain away, but it does aid in formulating a plan for overcoming it.

Another significant factor implied in the belief in God is that here is a source of power to give strength for any situations that may arise in our lives. Human existence is fraught with problems, difficult situations, frustrations, and sufferings. Sometimes these are very severe and disorganizing to us. Our faith assures us that in God we have a power sufficient for all our needs. This power is readily available to all who call upon him. No matter what the circumstance may be, it is well within our ability to face it and to overcome it. Job, in his terrible suffering, couldn't give a reasoned answer to his problems, but he could find in God the ultimate source of life, and the power to suffer without being overwhelmed.

This power is released to us through response to our prayers. When we feel the need for companionship or strength, we have the instrument of prayer, which we can use in the full assurance that God hears prayers and answers. He is concerned about the needs of each of us, and his power is available to help meet them. Prayer is choosing the help of God in the full expectation that our quest will be successful. The nature and interests of God are such that he can and will respond.

An active prayer life is the vehicle of appropriating God's help, and yet for so many of us it is an unsatisfactory experience. Prayer has given strength to the great Christians of all ages, yet many people have tried it and found it unrewarding and have given it up. Others have been unsure as to how to start, so they have never really prayed. How can we appropriate for ourselves this valuable instrument?

For those who find themselves unable to have a rewarding prayer experience, at least temporarily during the shock of grief, there is help in using the great prayers of others. By reading prayers that have expressed the spiritual hungers of the generations we are gradually enabled to make those prayers our own, and as we do so, response begins to come. The reading of Scripture, poetry, or prose passages from literature that have expressed the grief and faith of others also enables us to establish that contact with God which forms the foundation for an adequate prayer life. Ultimately, however, we shall want to come to the personal communion embodied in our own spontaneous prayers. This may require discipline and patience at first. As we choose a time and a place to bring our thoughts and needs to God, however, we shall gradually find ourselves able to make our prayers and to receive the communion and strength which they bring.

A further help that our religion has to offer is the practice of confession. In grief, or at any time when we become involved in feelings of guilt, we have the instrument of confession for overcoming them. The necessity for the expression and confession of these guilt feelings, if we are to overcome them and return to emotional health, is realized more fully now than ever before.

Confession has been made a part of the required practice for Roman Catholics and is found in the liturgies of some Protestant groups. Public confession was the practice of midweek prayer meetings of another day. No doubt these had some therapeutic value, but they were likely to be superficial and soothing rather than purging and reconstructing. Too often they were made the tool of political control, or opened the confessee to the vindictiveness or the judgments of the confessor. The shortcomings of these procedures are rapidly being overcome now by the increased interest in personal counseling on the part of Protestant ministers. They are learning new skills, and giving more time to the service of individuals who are interested in coming to them.

Confession that we make to Protestant ministers is freely given, and therefore more likely to be wholehearted. It is when we ourselves feel the need for release that we of our own free will go to make our confession. We can tell all we wish to tell at the time, but we are under no coercion to tell that which we want to keep secret. It is only our own need frankly to face our guilt feelings that drives us to make full and open confession of all that is troubling us. This task is made easier by the assurance that the one whom we have chosen as our confidant will not pass judgment upon us. Even when our confession involves matters that we know to be against his moral code, our trust is that he will aid us in spiritual growth rather than add to our burden by passing judgment upon us.

For the many people the making of a clear and frank confession requires the seeking out of a tangible, human confessor. Nevertheless, it is important that both we and our confessor remember that real confession is being made unto God. He is the one whom we must honestly face. Our confession doesn't increase his knowledge, but it does bring us to an honest owning of our error, and to a real desire for the renewal of a right spirit within. In situations where there is an opportunity to right a wrong, a true desire to do so is called for. This is not possible, however, in the case of grief, and the desire is for a forgiveness that will bring us to greater spiritual maturity. It is for a forgiveness that assures us that past irredeemable errors need not be a burden on us any longer, but can be cleared away.

Christian confession gains point beyond the psychological release of emotional tension in the assurance which we have that when we make full and honest confession, God will forgive us our sins. This belief is especially helpful in situations such as grief, where corrective action is impossible. When the bereaved is overwhelmed by guilt feelings, whether for real or fancied wrongs done the deceased, there is no opportunity to make restitution. Our only salvation is to believe that there is divine forgiveness. When we are convinced of divine forgiveness, then we can go the final step of forgiving ourselves. Without this latter step there can be no emotional health. When, however, we can accept ourselves as we are, in full confidence that God can make us whole, then we are on the road to spiritual maturity.

Yet another resource that religion has to offer to the bereaved is a purpose in life. When our lives have been closely tied to another individual and our values centered in him, bereavement may seem to take away all values and all purpose in living. This makes for a lack of zest in living and a meaninglessness of one's activities. Religion gives purpose to life.

Christian purpose includes living life to the full for its own sake. This is unrelated to business or material success or even to freedom from sorrow and suffering. In fact it might well be the bearing of tribulations and frustrations in a victorious manner. It is the taking of life's experiences as they come and using them to shape one's character and personality into a well-integrated life. Each of us is of value in his own right, and in spite of our loss, we have a work to do in fulfilling our own mission in life.

The word "growth" probably sums up the purpose basic for each of us. This is that each of us may become a more mature individual. There is no indication that the intention of God for us is that we should have an easy time in life, or that we should have prosperity, or popularity, or power over our fellow men. It would seem, rather, that life is made a struggle, that we might grow in body and soul. This is brought about through successfully meeting suffering and sorrow. It is also brought about through creative activity. The struggle for our daily bread may become tedious at times, but it also helps us to become more adult. If circumstances are such that we do not find it necessary to earn a living, then other activities, such as painting or teaching a Sunday school class, that challenge our abilities to greater and greater efforts will serve the purpose. Our religion, by stressing the creative purpose of life, gives us strength for living.

When the need for creative activity is turned outward toward others, it is embodied in the service motive. Our faith makes strong claims upon us to consider the needs of our fellow men. These needs range all the way from the elemental requirements for food and drink to the need for spiritual food to nourish one's soul. We are to be on the alert to observe where these needs are acute, and to be ready to do what we can in rendering service accordingly.

When we accede to this service motive as it is embodied in our religion, the result is new growth and new life for us. Grief, for example, loses its power when our loneliness is overcome by a new concern for others. As we become involved in doing good for others, we come to see and to appreciate the good that is present in our own lives. Accepting service for others turns us from dwelling in the arid land of self-concern and carries us to the lush country of common enterprise.

A young woman lost her physician husband in the prime of life. She had had everything: a good family, a good home, money, and high social position. After her bereavement she still had all except her husband. Nevertheless, in spite of all her friends could do, she headed for a nervous breakdown. Finally, her physician recommended that she find some service project to which she could give her energies. The result was a lay ministry in a rural church, with a complete regaining of health and a new enthusiasm for living.

A still further resource that religion has to offer to us in bereavement is church fellowship. In grief we suffer from loneliness, and from the loss of fellowship with the deceased. No individual or group can replace our beloved, but they can help to fill the empty space which he left. In the fellowship of worship there is strength as we join with others in communion with God. Here we can find common cause with others as we have fellowship on life's deepest plane.

The fellowship of the church is not limited to the worship service, however. It becomes more intimate and more active in smaller informal groups. In clubs, discussion groups, or socials there is more opportunity for direct interaction with others. In the church is the best place for many of us to find the healing fellowship of congenial persons.

WE SHALL BE COMFORTED

SOME WHO READ earlier chapters will say, "But I know someone who didn't give way to grief in that way," or, "Not me; I'm not a child that I should not keep my chin up when bereavement comes." Grief can be denied or delayed, and many there are who do it. For some this is an unconscious maneuver, while for others it is a deliberate action. The pain of loneliness drives many to crowd out the memories that cause it. Many seek through absorption in work to forget their sorrows. Others just seek to be brave. No man wants to be called "sissy," and so many suppress all emotions and face their friends and neighbors with a brave front. Still others, trained in Christian stoicism, regard all show of sorrow as a lack of faith. These not only suppress the expression of the sorrow that they feel, but are likely to deny to themselves the need for such expression.

Grief can be delayed or denied, but this is a perilous course. Grief is a negative emotion, and when a negative emotion is repressed, it is not thereby disposed of. It is pushed down into the unconscious, where it remains as powerful and as destructive as ever. This fact escapes many people, because the emotion may disguise itself until the individual does not realize what the destructive force is that is working in him. Only when he has worked through his secondary symptoms with a counselor does he come to the realization as to what the original source of his trouble really is. Thus many people suppress grief and think they get away with it, but they seldom do. One aware of this fact finds many examples of it in any community.

Many of the best illustrations cannot be used because they involve confidences that cannot be revealed. Some stories, though, can be suggested. There is the woman who gave many years to the care of her very aged mother. When the mother finally died, the daughter was dry-eyed. The mother had been very ill and very much of a care. The daughter considered death as a blessing and a relief to both. She was very tired, and after the funeral went away for a prolonged vacation and rest. She returned and made various attempts at re-establishing herself, but she rapidly wasted away and died. She never conquered her grief; her grief conquered her.

Another and younger woman was called to the care of her mother from a good teaching position in a leading college. She was still relatively young when her mother died, but she never again was the same. She took on no creative employment after this. Property that she inherited was allowed to become cluttered, and even the room in which she spent most of her time was piled thick with dust. Her clothes were coarse, and served her on those rare occasions when she joined social gatherings as well as at home. Her mind remained alert with books, but in the practical and social affairs of everyday life she was lost.

One young woman had spent much time and money in seeking treatment for hypertension due to nervousness, a condition which her mother stated was just the opposite of her nature as a girl. Counseling unveiled the fact that the condition began and had continually intensified since a stillbirth. A similar event was found to lie back of the hostility that another woman expressed toward God and his church, even though in her younger years this woman had been active in Sunday school and the church.

The death of his wife changed one pleasant and sociable man into a belligerent person, unable to get along with others either at work or at home. The death of a young son caused another to lose his interest in his work and to neglect his home. Grief which we thought we had eluded often proves to be present in unrecognized but very diabolical forms. Complete character changes are often brought about by this force which we deny.

Some of the false fronts grief has been found to wear merit our consideration. If we realize what the attempt to deny grief has done to others, we shall be more willing to face our own grief. Furthermore, if we realize what lies back of some of the characteristics we find in others, we shall be helped to be more patient and wise in our relationships to them. When we realize that our friend's irritability is due, not to maliciousness, but to grief, we can more readily make allowances for him, and even help him over the rough spots of his daily associations with others. When we realize that the hostility that a woman has for the church is not due to any fault she has found in the church, nor yet to any perversion on her part, but to the bitterness of her grief, then we can be patient with her, help her to see where the real source of her difficulty is, and through patience and tact win her back to peace with herself and with her fellow men and with her God.

The first of these false fronts for our consideration is vivaciousness. Instead of following the expected pattern of sorrow and depression, the person seems to have received new life. Where he may have been quiet and easygoing before, now he seems to be filled with enthusiasm and energy. He is the life of the party, and takes in all the parties. He has big ideas for his job, or for new jobs that he wants to undertake. He is optimistic, gay, and constantly on the go — as long as the spell lasts, as long as he can delay his grief.

Probably the most common false front worn by grief is irritability. Instead of acknowledging his grief and allowing himself to carry through with the pain involved, the bereaved may become aggressive and hostile to all comers. The parent becomes irritated with his children, so that any noise is made a major issue, or ordinary family activities become matters of contention. The workman may become resentful of the instructions of his boss and toward the usual competition of his fellow workers. In all contacts with other persons there may be a " chip on the shoulder " attitude which leads to constant friction and unpleasantness.

A variation of this general irritability may be hostility toward one particular individual. The attending physician is a favorite target. We often expect too much of our physician. We expect him to work magic which he is not capable of performing, and blame him for his failure. It is easy to convince ourselves that if the physician had come sooner, or done differently, death of our loved one might not have occurred. Physicians become accustomed to expressions of hostility for which there is no justification. Others besides the physician may get the blame. In an automobile accident the driver of the other car is the obvious villain. One's husband may get the blame for not calling a physician to see the child sooner, or one's wife may be accused of lack of sufficient care for the now lost infant. If the individual who arouses our hostility is the driver of the other car, whom we do not know or never see, the results may not be a serious disruption in relationships, but if the enemy is within one's own household, the results may be of greater consequence. In any case there is a serious problem within the bereaved himself.

A less common, but nevertheless real, possibility is the false front of identification with the deceased individual. A woman may cover up her grief by taking on mannerisms that belonged to her husband. She may assume his role in the home, and even attempt to fit into his business position, even though she is wholly unfitted for this. A man may appear at his physician's office complaining of the same heart symptoms of which his now deceased father complained, even though with the son there is no physical basis for the complaint whatever. This is not conscious imitation of the deceased. The bereaved is often very reluctant to recognize that he is assuming the role of the departed. If he does, he is likely to be shocked by the discovery. This is a false front which the grief he denied wears so that it can come to expression, if not openly, then disguised.

Physical illness may turn out to be a false front for grief. A woman who had been under treatment for a period of years for high blood pressure due to nerves was found to have developed her condition immediately following the death of an infant child. Even such diseases as asthma, arthritis, rheumatism, and colitis have been found at times to be nervous in origin, and sometimes the nervous condition has been traced to suppressed grief.

Another false front of grief is false grief. A man, for example, may lose his wife, and bear up like a true soldier. He is admired for his courage and control. Then a few years later a casual acquaintance dies and our hero has a strong grief reaction. Neighbors are amazed to learn that the deceased meant so much to him. He didn't. When we get beneath this false grief, we find that our friend is really doing belated grieving for his wife. Grief has patience, but it can't be denied its ultimate expression in some form or other.

Rare, but unfortunately real, is the false front of mental depression. This is real mental illness, and much too high a price to pay for avoidance of the pain of loneliness in fresh grief or for the dubious flattery of friends because of a brave front when loved ones die. There is no comfort for those who do not mourn.

For all these false fronts there is only one final solution. That is to go back and do the mourning that we should have done in the first place. The longer our grief is delayed, the more painful it is when it does come out. The more set these false fronts become, the more reluctant they are to give way to health which is our due when grief work is properly done.

When we mourn, we shall be comforted. The pain of sobbing is well worth while because of the achievement of the release of emotional tension. It may be unpleasant for a short time, but the value received in getting rid of the pain and avoidance of depression later on is more than sufficient compensation. These more than compensate, too, for any loss of face that we may suffer before those who have the mistaken notion that real mourning is immature. Our faith is all on the side of passing through unpleasant experiences to fuller life on the other side.

When we mourn, we are imperceptibly getting rid of the pain of loneliness. The second period of sobbing may not seem to be milder than the first, but in a few days the acuteness of it will be dulled, and in the end even when we keep the form, the pain will be slight, and erelong the periods of sobbing will be rare.

Between the periods of sobbing we shall want to express our sense of loss and sorrow. This will bring us face to face with the fact of our loss. As human personalities we can stand a great deal in the way of emotional shock, but the one thing that gets us into trouble is deceit. When we honestly face and accept a fact, no matter how distressing, the immediate shock can be accommodated without dire consequences, but when we try to evade or suppress unpleasant realities, then we are in for emotional disturbances. When we express our sense of loss and sorrow, the reality of it is fully established, it is accepted, and it is overcome.

There is release in the expression of hostility. If we try to suppress the anger that we feel toward the deceased, it remains as a bottled-up pressure, but if we find an adequate outlet, we can be freed from the tyranny of it. Emotional tensions that have been building up over the years can be disposed of by verbal expression to a counselor. When our expression is made and the tension is released, we begin to see the acts that antagonized us in their true proportion. They lose their grip on us and begin to seem of less and less significance, until finally they are dissolved in the general background of the larger memories of our beloved. True, failures and faults will not be forgotten, but their threat to us will have been dissipated. Our tolerance and spirit of forgiveness will have risen above any wrong we may have suffered.

Furthermore, our feelings of guilt can be conquered. The tension surrounding them will be reduced, and they can be brought into true perspective. If they are unreasonable, they will gradually so appear. If they are justified, they can be honestly faced, lead to a spirit of true contrition, and thence to the assurance of forgiveness with all the freedom and release that that means.

When we have freed ourselves from the acute pain of the first loneliness and shock, then we are ready to enlarge our understanding of the meaning of life and death. Securing release from the pain of loss is not an act of disrespect to our loved one. It frees us for a more wholesome reverence. We are then ready to face and to understand the implications of our belief in immortality. The pain of separation is soothed by the assurance that our loved one has entered into an expanded life.

It is clear, furthermore, that our pain is for our own loneliness, and not for harm coming to one for whom we care. This enables us to bear our pain better, and to feel free to extricate ourselves from it. Still further, it gives us the consolation of the implications of the assurance that our loved one is not gone, but gone before. The separation is real, but it is not permanent. Our beloved has arrived before us at one of the major stepping-stones of life, but we too shall undergo this universal experience, and shall know as we are known.

Having mourned and been comforted ourselves, we are better prepared to comfort others in their time of sorrow. Our sympathy will be more real when we know from experience something of what the other person is going through. Having mourned ourselves, our poise in the presence of the sobbing of others will be more supporting and reassuring. Having passed through the waters ourselves, we can witness more effectively to the promise that " they shall not overflow thee." We can speak from experience and know that, even though the grief of the moment is all-consuming, it too shall pass, and that they who mourn shall be comforted.

PART TWO

WORDS OF COMFORT

OLD TESTAMENT

THE eternal God is thy refuge,
   And underneath are the everlasting arms.
                    — *Deuteronomy 33:27.*

Be strong and of a good courage; be not afraid, neither be thou dismayed: for the Lord thy God is with thee withersoever thou goest.

                    — *Joshua 1:9.*

And it came to pass on the seventh day, that the child died. And the servants of David feared to tell him that the child was dead: for they said, Behold, while the child was yet alive, we spake unto him, and he would not hearken unto our voice: how will he then vex himself, if we tell him that the child is dead? But when David saw that his servants whispered, David perceived that the child was dead: therefore David said unto his servants, Is the child dead? And they said, He is dead. Then David arose from the earth, and washed, and anointed himself, and changed his apparel, and came into the house of the Lord, and worshipped: then he came to his own house; and when he required, they set bread before him, and he did eat. Then said his servants unto him, What thing is this that thou hast done? thou didst fast and weep for the child, while it was alive; but when the child was dead, thou didst rise and eat bread. And he said, While the child was yet alive, I fasted and wept: for I said, Who can tell whether God will be gracious to me, that the child may live? But now he is dead, wherefore should I fast? can I bring him back again? I shall go to him, but he shall not return to me.

— II Samuel 12:18–23.

I have set the Lord always before me:
Because he is at my right hand, I shall not be moved.

— Psalm 16:8.

The Lord is my shepherd; I shall not want.
He maketh me to lie down in green pastures:
He leadeth me beside the still waters.
He restoreth my soul:
He leadeth me in the paths of righteousness for his name's sake.
Yea, though I walk through the valley of the shadow of death,
I will fear no evil: for thou art with me;
Thy rod and thy staff they comfort me.
Thou preparest a table before me in the presence of mine enemies:
Thou anointest my head with oil; my cup runneth over.
Surely goodness and mercy shall follow me all the days of my life:
And I will dwell in the house of the Lord for ever.

— Psalm 23.

The Lord is my light and my salvation; whom shall I fear?
The Lord is the strength of my life; of whom shall I be afraid?
When the wicked, even mine enemies and my foes,
Came upon me to eat up my flesh,
They stumbled and fell.

Though a host should encamp against me,
My heart shall not fear:
Though war should rise against me,
In this will I be confident.
One thing have I desired of the Lord, that will I seek after;
That I may dwell in the house of the Lord all the days of my
    life,
To behold the beauty of the Lord, and to inquire in his temple.
For in the time of trouble he shall hide me in his pavilion:
In the secret of his tabernacle shall he hide me;
He shall set me up upon a rock.
And now shall mine head be lifted up above mine enemies
    round about me:
Therefore will I offer in his tabernacle sacrifices of joy;
I will sing, yea, I will sing praises unto the Lord.
Hear, O Lord, when I cry with my voice:
Have mercy also upon me, and answer me.
When thou saidst, Seek ye my face;
My heart said unto thee,
Thy face, Lord, will I seek.
Hide not thy face far from me;
Put not thy servant away in anger:
Thou hast been my help;
Leave me not, neither forsake me,
O God of my salvation.
When my father and my mother forsake me,
Then the Lord will take me up.

—Psalm 27:1-10.

As the hart panteth after the water brooks,
So panteth my soul after thee, O God.
My soul thirsteth for God, for the living God:
When shall I come and appear before God?

My tears have been my meat day and night,
While they continually say unto me, Where is thy God?
When I remember these things, I pour out my soul in me:
For I had gone with the multitude, I went with them to the
    house of God,
With the voice of joy and praise, with a multitude that kept
    holyday.

— Psalm 42:1-4.

God is our refuge and strength,
A very present help in trouble.
Therefore will not we fear, though the earth be removed,
And though the mountains be carried into the midst of the sea;
Though the waters thereof roar and be troubled,
Though the mountains shake with the swelling thereof.
There is a river, the streams whereof shall make glad the city
    of God,
The holy place of the tabernacles of the Most High.
God is in the midst of her; she shall not be moved:
God shall help her, and that right early.
The heathen raged, the kingdoms were moved:
He uttered his voice, the earth melted.
The Lord of hosts is with us;
The God of Jacob is our refuge.
Come, behold the works of the Lord,
What desolations he hath made in the earth.
He maketh wars to cease unto the end of the earth;
He breaketh the bow, and cutteth the spear in sunder;
He burneth the chariot in the fire.
Be still, and know that I am God:
I will be exalted among the heathen, I will be exalted in the
    earth.

The Lord of hosts is with us;
The God of Jacob is our refuge.

— Psalm 46.

Lord, thou hast been our dwelling place in all generations.
Before the mountains were brought forth,
Or ever thou hadst formed the earth and the world,
Even from everlasting to everlasting, thou art God.

— Psalm 90:1, 2.

He that dwelleth in the secret place of the Most High
Shall abide under the shadow of the Almighty.
I will say of the Lord, He is my refuge and my fortress:
My God; in him will I trust.
Surely he shall deliver thee from the snare of the fowler,
And from the noisome pestilence.
He shall cover thee with his feathers,
And under his wings shalt thou trust:
His truth shall be thy shield and buckler.
Thou shalt not be afraid for the terror by night;
Nor for the arrow that flieth by day;
Nor for the pestilence that walketh in darkness;
Nor for the destruction that wasteth at noonday.
A thousand shall fall at thy side,
And ten thousand at thy right hand;
But it shall not come nigh thee.
Only with thine eyes shalt thou behold
And see the reward of the wicked.
Because thou hast made the Lord, which is my refuge,
Even the Most High, thy habitation;
There shall no evil befall thee,
Neither shall any plague come nigh thy dwelling.

For he shall give his angels charge over thee,
To keep thee in all thy ways.
They shall bear thee up in their hands,
Lest thou dash thy foot against a stone.
Thou shalt tread upon the lion and adder:
The young lion and the dragon shalt thou trample under feet.
Because he hath set his love upon me, therefore will I deliver
    him:
I will set him on high, because he hath known my name.
He shall call upon me, and I will answer him:
I will be with him in trouble;
I will deliver him, and honor him.
With long life will I satisfy him,
And show him my salvation.

—Psalm 91.

I will lift up mine eyes unto the hills,
From whence cometh my help.
My help cometh from the Lord,
Which made heaven and earth.
He will not suffer thy foot to be moved:
He that keepeth thee will not slumber.
Behold, he that keepeth Israel
Shall neither slumber nor sleep.
The Lord is thy keeper:
The Lord is thy shade upon thy right hand.
The sun shall not smite thee by day,
Nor the moon by night.
The Lord shall preserve thee from all evil:
He shall preserve thy soul.
The Lord shall preserve thy going out and thy coming in
From this time forth, and even for evermore.

—Psalm 121.

He will swallow up death in victory;
And the Lord God will wipe away tears from off all faces;
And the rebuke of his people shall he take away from off all
    the earth:
For the Lord hath spoken it.
And it shall be said in that day,
Lo, this is our God;
We have waited for him, and he will save us:
This is the Lord; we have waited for him,
We will be glad and rejoice in his salvation.

                                                   —Isaiah 25:8, 9.

Thou wilt keep him in perfect peace, whose mind is stayed on
    thee:
Because he trusteth in thee.

                                                   —Isaiah 26:3.

Hast thou not known? hast thou not heard,
That the everlasting God, the Lord,
The Creator of the ends of the earth,
Fainteth not, neither is weary?
There is no searching of his understanding.
He giveth power to the faint;
And to them that have no might he increaseth strength.
Even the youths shall faint and be weary,
And the young men shall utterly fall:
But they that wait upon the Lord shall renew their strength;
They shall mount up with wings as eagles;
They shall run, and not be weary;
And they shall walk, and not faint.

                                              —Isaiah 40:28–31.

For I the Lord thy God
Will hold thy right hand,
Saying unto thee, Fear not;
I will help thee.

—*Isaiah 41:13.*

When thou passest through the waters, I will be with thee;
And through the rivers, they shall not overflow thee:
When thou walkest through the fire, thou shalt not be burned;
Neither shall the flame kindle upon thee.

—*Isaiah 43:2.*

NEW TESTAMENT

BLESSED are they that mourn: for they shall be comforted.

— Matthew 5:4.

Come unto me, all ye that labor and are heavy laden, and I will give you rest.

— Matthew 11:28.

For God so loved the world, that he gave his only begotten Son, that whosoever believeth in him should not perish, but have everlasting life.

— John 3:16.

Jesus said unto her, I am the resurrection, and the life: he that believeth in me, though he were dead, yet shall he live: and whosoever liveth and believeth in me shall never die.

— John 11:25, 26.

Let not your heart be troubled: ye believe in God, believe also in me. In my Father's house are many mansions: if it were not so, I would have told you. I go to prepare a place for you. And if I go and prepare a place for you, I will come again, and receive you unto myself; that where I am, there ye may be also. And whither I go ye know, and the way ye know.

Thomas saith unto him, Lord, we know not whither thou goest; and how can we know the way? Jesus saith unto him, I am the way, the truth, and the life: no man cometh unto the Father, but by me. If ye had known me, ye should have known my Father also: and from henceforth ye know him, and have seen him.

Philip saith unto him, Lord, show us the Father, and it sufficeth us. Jesus saith unto him, Have I been so long time with you, and yet hast thou not known me, Philip? he that hath seen me hath seen the Father; and how sayest thou then, Show us the Father? Believest thou not that I am in the Father, and the Father in me? the words that I speak unto you I speak not of myself: but the Father that dwelleth in me, he doeth the works. Believe me that I am in the Father, and the Father in me: or else believe me for the very works' sake.

—John 14:1-11.

I will not leave you comfortless: I will come to you. Yet a little while, and the world seeth me no more; but ye see me: because I live, ye shall live also. At that day ye shall know that I am in my Father, and ye in me, and I in you. He that hath my commandments, and keepeth them, he it is that loveth me: and he that loveth me shall be loved of my Father, and I will love him, and will manifest myself to him.

—John 14:18-21.

In the world ye shall have tribulation: but be of good cheer; I have overcome the world.

—John 16:33.

Therefore being justified by faith, we have peace with God through our Lord Jesus Christ: by whom also we have access by faith into this grace wherein we stand, and rejoice in hope of the glory of God. And not only so, but we glory in tribulations also; knowing that tribulation worketh patience; and patience, experience; and experience, hope: and hope maketh not ashamed; because the love of God is shed abroad in our hearts by the Holy Ghost which is given unto us.

— Romans 5:1–5.

For I am persuaded, that neither death, nor life, nor angels, nor principalities, nor powers, nor things present, nor things to come, nor height, nor depth, nor any other creature, shall be able to separate us from the love of God, which is in Christ Jesus our Lord.

— Romans 8:38, 39.

For none of us liveth to himself, and no man dieth to himself. For whether we live, we live unto the Lord; and whether we die, we die unto the Lord: whether we live therefore, or die, we are the Lord's.

— Romans 14:7, 8.

But now is Christ risen from the dead, and become the first-fruits of them that slept. For since by man came death, by man came also the resurrection of the dead. For as in Adam all die, even so in Christ shall all be made alive. But every man in his own order: Christ the firstfruits; afterward they that are Christ's at his coming. Then cometh the end, when he shall have delivered up the kingdom to God, even the Father; when he shall have put down all rule, and all authority and power. For he must reign, till he hath put all enemies under his feet. The last enemy that shall be destroyed is death. For he hath put all things under his feet. But when he saith, All things are put under him, it is manifest that he is excepted, which did put all things under him. And when all things shall be subdued unto him, then shall the Son also himself be subject unto him that put all things under him, that God may be all in all. . . .

But some man will say, How are the dead raised up? and with what body do they come? Thou fool, that which thou sowest is not quickened, except it die: and that which thou sowest, thou sowest not that body that shall be, but bare grain, it may chance of wheat, or of some other grain: but God giveth it a body as it hath pleased him, and to every seed his own body. All flesh is not the same flesh: but there is one kind of flesh of men, another flesh of beasts, another of fishes, and another of birds. There are also celestial bodies, and bodies terrestrial: but the glory of the celestial is one, and the glory of the terrestrial is another. There is one glory of the sun, and another glory of the moon, and another glory of the stars; for one star differeth from another star in glory.

So also is the resurrection of the dead. It is sown in corruption, it is raised in incorruption: it is sown in dishonor, it is raised in glory: it is sown in weakness, it is raised in power: it is sown a natural body, it is raised a spiritual body. There is a natural body, and there is a spiritual body. And so it is written, The first man Adam was made a living soul; the last Adam was made a quickening spirit. Howbeit that was not first which is spiritual, but that which is natural; and afterward that which is spiritual. The first man is of the earth, earthy: the second man is the Lord from heaven. As is the earthy, such are they also that are earthy: and as is the heavenly, such are they also that are heavenly. And as we have borne the image of the earthy, we shall also bear the image of the heavenly.

Now this I say, brethren, that flesh and blood cannot inherit the kingdom of God; neither doth corruption inherit incorruption. . . . For this corruptible must put on incorruption, and this mortal must put on immortality. So when this corruptible shall have put on incorruption, and this mortal shall have put on immortality, then shall be brought to pass the saying that is written,

> Death is swallowed up in victory.
> O death, where is thy sting?
> O grave, where is thy victory?

The sting of death is sin; and the strength of sin is the law. But thanks be to God, which giveth us the victory through our Lord Jesus Christ.

Therefore, my beloved brethren, be ye steadfast, unmovable, always abounding in the work of the Lord, forasmuch as ye know that your labor is not in vain in the Lord.

—I Corinthians 15:20-28, 35-50, 53-58.

Blessed be God, even the Father of our Lord Jesus Christ, the Father of mercies, and the God of all comfort; who comforteth us in all our tribulation, that we may be able to comfort them which are in any trouble, by the comfort wherewith we ourselves are comforted of God. For as the sufferings of Christ abound in us, so our consolation also aboundeth by Christ.

—II Corinthians 1:3-5.

We also believe, and therefore speak; knowing that he which raised up the Lord Jesus shall raise up us also by Jesus, and shall present us with you. . . .

For which cause we faint not; but though our outward man perish, yet the inward man is renewed day by day. For our light affliction, which is but for a moment, worketh for us a far more exceeding and eternal weight of glory; while we look not at the things which are seen, but at things which are not seen: for the things which are seen are temporal; but the things which are not seen are eternal.

— II Corinthians 4:13, 14, 16–18.

For we know that, if our earthly house of this tabernacle were dissolved, we have a building of God, a house not made with hands, eternal in the heavens. For in this we groan, earnestly desiring to be clothed upon with our house which is from heaven: if so be that being clothed we shall not be found naked. For we that are in this tabernacle do groan, being burdened: not for that we would be unclothed, but clothed upon, that mortality might be swallowed up of life. Now he that hath wrought us for the selfsame thing is God, who also hath given unto us the earnest of the Spirit. Therefore we are always confident, knowing that, whilst we are at home in the body, we are absent from the Lord: (for we walk by faith, not by sight:) we are confident, I say, and willing rather to be absent from the body, and to be present with the Lord.

— II Corinthians 5:1–8.

I can do all things through Christ which strengtheneth me.

— Philippians 4:13.

But I would not have you to be ignorant, brethren, concerning them which are asleep, that ye sorrow not, even as others which have no hope. For if we believe that Jesus died and rose again, even so them also which sleep in Jesus will God bring with him.

— I Thessalonians 4:13, 14.

Be not thou therefore ashamed of the testimony of our Lord, nor of me his prisoner: but be thou partaker of the afflictions of the gospel according to the power of God; who hath saved us, and called us with a holy calling, not according to our works, but according to his own purpose and grace, which was given us in Christ Jesus before the world began; but is now made manifest by the appearing of our Saviour Jesus Christ, who hath abolished death, and hath brought life and immortality to light through the gospel.

—II Timothy 1:8–10.

And I saw a new heaven and a new earth: for the first heaven and the first earth were passed away; and there was no more sea. And I John saw the holy city, new Jerusalem, coming down from God out of heaven, prepared as a bride adorned for her husband. And I heard a great voice out of heaven saying, Behold, the tabernacle of God is with men, and he will dwell with them, and they shall be his people, and God himself shall be with them, and be their God. And God shall wipe away all tears from their eyes; and there shall be no more death, neither sorrow, nor crying, neither shall there be any more pain: for the former things are passed away.

And he that sat upon the throne said, Behold, I make all things new. And he said unto me, Write: for these words are true and faithful. And he said unto me, It is done. I am Alpha and Omega, the beginning and the end. I will give unto him that is athirst of the fountain of the water of life freely. He that overcometh shall inherit all things; and I will be his God, and he shall be my son.

—Revelation 21:1–7.

PRAYERS

Prayer of Hope

ETERNAL FATHER, Thou who art from everlasting to everlasting the same and changest not: we rejoice in the constancy of Thy being and Thy watchful care over us. We thank Thee for the assurance that we do not build for the moment only to see the fruits of our labors wiped away, but that when we labor in Thee we build for eternity. We thank Thee that Thy laws do not change, that what is right and good and true today will be for ever so. Help us to see those things that are eternal, that we may give our efforts not only to the living of this life to the full, but at the same time to the preparation for that expanded life which is to come. Amen.

— W. F. R.

Prayer with a Bereaved Person

Almighty and ever-present God,
Thou in whom we live and move and have our being:
Draw near unto us, that we may know the support of Thy
    affection;
Bless this one [these persons] through these days and renew
    him [them] in faith.
May the affection he has known bear him up through the days
    ahead.

May his loneliness give way to fellowship,
And may his regrets give way to hope;
Overshadow his despair with a divine peace.
Enable him to know that we commune with our loved ones
Who are gone before us as we commune with Thee.
May he know that dying is a moving toward a fuller life with
    Thee.
May we not look longingly back at our yesterdays,
But move forward eagerly toward our tomorrows
In faith and hope and confidence,
Through the grace and love we know in Christ Jesus.   Amen.
                                        — *Russell Dicks.*

Prayer in Bereavement

O God, help me to think of Thee in this bitter trial. Thou
knowest how my heart is rent with grief. In my weakness,
tested so severely in soul by this visitation, I cry unto Thee,
Father of all life; give me fortitude to say with Thy servant
Job: "The Lord hath given; the Lord hath taken away;
blessed be the name of the Lord."

Forgive the thoughts of my rebellious soul. Pardon me in
these first hours of my grief, if I question Thy wisdom and
exercise myself in things too high for me. Grant me strength
to rise above this trial, to bear with humility life's sorrows and
disappointments. Be nigh unto me, O God. Bring consolation
and peace to my soul.

Praised art Thou, O God, who comfortest the mourners.
                        — *The Union Prayer-Book for Jewish Worship.*

O Almighty God, the God of spirits of all flesh, who by a
voice from heaven didst proclaim, Blessed are the dead who

die in the Lord: Multiply, we beseech thee, to those who rest in Jesus, the manifold blessings of thy love, that the good work which thou didst begin in them may be perfected unto the day of Jesus Christ. And of thy mercy, O heavenly Father, vouchsafe that we, who now serve thee here on earth, may at last, together with them, be found meet to be partakers of the inheritance of the saints in the light; for the sake of the same thy Son, Jesus Christ, our Lord and Saviour. Amen.

— *The Scottish Book of Common Prayer.*

Almighty and everlasting God, the comfort of the sad, the strength of sufferers; let the prayers of those that cry out of any tribulation come unto Thee; that all may find Thy Spirit giving them victory in their afflictions; through Christ our Lord. Amen.

— *The Book of Common Worship, Revised.*

Thanks be to Thee, O God, that Thy Son, Jesus Christ our Lord, conquered death and brought life and immortality to light through the gospel. We praise Thee for His assurance of Thy house of many mansions, where He has prepared a place for us, that where He is, there we may be also. . . . Wherefore we rejoice in this hour for those whom we have lost on earth, but who are now with Thee. . . . By Thy grace comfort our hearts with the thought of their safety and joy, and help us so to walk before Thee in faith and love, that in Thy good time, we may be joined to them in Thy heavenly presence evermore; through Jesus Christ our Lord. Amen.

— *The Book of Common Worship, Revised.*

Almighty God, Father of mercies and giver of all comfort, deal graciously, we pray Thee, with all those who mourn, that, casting every care on Thee, they may know the consolation of Thy love; through Jesus Christ our Lord. Amen.

— The Book of Common Prayer.

A Prayer

O Lord, our Heavenly Father, almighty and most merciful God, in whose hands are life and death, who givest and takest away, castest down, and raisest up, look with mercy on the suffering of Thy unworthy servant, and speak peace to my troubled soul. . . . Release me from my sorrow, fill me with just hopes, true faith, and holy consolations, and enable me to do my duty in that state of life to which Thou hast been pleased to call me, without disturbance from fruitless grief, or tumultuous imaginations; that in all my thoughts, words, and actions, I may glorify Thy holy Name, and finally obtain, what I hope Thou hast granted to Thy departed servant, ever-lasting joy and felicity.

—Samuel Johnson,

INSPIRED THOUGHTS

Immortal Child

THOU HAST NOT lost thy son, but bestowed him henceforward in eternity. Say not then, "I am no longer called 'father'"; for why art thou no longer called so, when thy son abideth? For surely thou didst not part with thy child, nor lose thy son. Rather thou hast gotten him, and hast him in greater safety. Wherefor, no longer shalt thou be called father now of a mortal child, but of an immortal. . . . Think not, because he is not present, that therefore he is lost; for had he been absent in a foreign land, the title of thy relationship had not gone from thee with his body. Do not then gaze on the countenance of what lieth there, for so thou dost but kindle afresh thy grief; but away with thy thought from that which lieth there, up to heaven. That is not thy child that is lying there; he has flown away and sprung aloft into boundless height. When, then, thou seest the eyes closed, the lips locked together, the body motionless, O be not these thy thoughts: "These lips no longer speak, these eyes no longer see, these feet no longer walk, but are on their way to corruption." O say not so; but say the reverse: "These lips shall speak better, these eyes shall see greater things, these feet shall mount upon the clouds, and this body . . . shall put on immortality, and I shall receive my son back more glorious."

— *Saint John Chrysostom.*

Consolation

All are not taken! there are left behind
Living beloveds tender looks to bring,
And make the daylight still a happy thing,
And tender voices, to make soft the wind.
But if it were not so — if I could find
No love in all the world for comforting,
Nor any path but hollowly did ring,
Where "dust to dust" the love from life disjoined —
And if before these sepulchers unmoving
I stood alone (as some forsaken lamb
Goes bleating up the moors in weary dearth),
Crying, "Where are ye, O my loved and loving?" . . .
I know a Voice would sound, "Daughter, I AM.
Can I suffice for heaven, and not for earth?"

       — *Elizabeth Barrett Browning.*

How to Bear Sorrow

I believe that the wisest plan is sometimes not to try to bear sorrow — as long as one is not crippled for one's everyday duties — but to give way to it utterly and freely. Perhaps sorrow is sent that we may give way to it, and in drinking the cup to the dregs, find some medicine in it itself, which we should not find if we began doctoring ourselves or letting others doctor us. If we say simply, "I am wretched — I ought to be wretched"; then we shall perhaps hear a voice: "Who made thee wretched but God? Then what can he mean but thy good?" And if the heart answers impatiently: "My good? I don't want it, I want my love," perhaps the voice may answer, "Then thou shalt have both in time."

       — *Charles Kingsley, in* Letters and Memories.

'Tis true, 'tis certain; man, tho' dead, retains
Part of himself; th' immortal mind remains.

— Homer.

What Is Steel?

" What is steel? " the Schoolman asked.
" Steel," I replied,
" Is iron dug from the vitals of the earth;
A few bits in a mighty mass of dirt,
Clinging rock and slate."
" And then? " he asked.
My lesson well I knew:
" By straining, sweating men this mass
Is taken to a noisy, fearsome Hell,
And there it faces agonies of excruciating pain —
Tortured in the crucible of flame
To burst forth strong and bright and true.
The rock and dust are slag,
Cast out. Not pure,
They have but hid the real. The steel is iron purified,
Pounded, crucified
Into perfection, to make
A rail as straight as light
O'er which men travel without fear
To do the blessed things of life;
A cable to bear the weight, mayhap
Of a majestic span;
A surgeon's scalpel, to cut away
Anguish and human pain."

— Stanley E. Anderson.

Comrades Still

To men filled with one overwhelming thought of the loss of those whom they will no more see or hear or touch, such an event as death seems to be the end of all comradeship. Yet to Christ this departure was to be the beginning of a relationship more intimate, more secure, and infinitely more fruitful. They should be comrades still. There should be no break in their relationship or in their work. "I go to the Father." "In my Father's house are many mansions . . . I go to prepare a place for you. And if I go and prepare a place for you, I come again, and will receive you unto myself; that where I am, there ye may be also." "Verily, verily, I say unto you, He that believeth on me, the works that I do shall he do also; and greater works than these shall he do; because I go unto the Father."

No wonder he recalled them to the truth of this going or departure which so filled their hearts with sorrow, and left them dumb even to ask the question, Whither goest thou? Everything depended upon that answer, for everything would find its explanation when once the direction and the issue of the journey was known.

— *John Maud, Bishop of Kensington,
in* Our Comradeship with the Blessed Dead.

O, yet we trust that somehow good
    Will be the final goal of ill,
    To pangs of nature, sins of will,
Defects of doubt, and taints of blood;

That nothing walks with aimless feet;
    That not one life shall be destroy'd,
    Or cast as rubbish to the void,
When God hath made the pile complete;

That not a worm is cloven in vain;
  That not a moth with vain desire
  Is shrivell'd in a fruitless fire,
Or but subserves another's gain.

Behold, we know not anything;
  I can but trust that good shall fall
  At last — far off — at last, to all,
And every winter change to spring.
       — *Alfred Lord Tennyson, in " In Memoriam."*

All mankinde is of one Author, and is one volume; when one Man dies, one Chapter is not torne out of the booke, but translated into a better language; and every Chapter must be so translated; God emploies several translators; some peeces are translated by age, some by sicknesse, some by warre, some by justice; but Gods hand is in every translation; and his hand shall binde up all our scattered leaves againe, for that Librairie where every booke shall lie open to one another.

       — *John Donne.*

Do not suppose, my dearest sons, that when I have left you I shall be nowhere and no one. Even when I was with you, you did not see my soul, but knew that it was in this body of mine from what I did. Believe, then, that it is still the same, even though you see it not. . . . For myself, I never could be persuaded that souls while in mortal bodies were alive, and died directly they left them; nor, in fact, that the soul lost all intelligence only when it left the unintelligent body. I believe rather that when, by being liberated from all corporeal admixture, it has begun to be pure and undefiled, it is then that it becomes wise.

       — *Cicero.*

Keep me from bitterness. It is so easy
To nurse sharp bitter thoughts each dull dark hour.
Against self-pity, Man of Sorrows, defend me,
With Thy deep sweetness and Thy gentle power.
And out of all this hurt of pain and heartbreak
Help me to harvest a new sympathy
For suffering human kind, a wiser pity
For those who lift a heavier cross with Thee.

— Anonymous.

The Summons

After this it was noised abroad that Mr. Valiant-for-truth
was taken with a summons by the same post as the other, and
had this for a token that the summons was true, That his
pitcher was broken at the fountain. When he understood it
he called for his friends, and told them of it. Then said he, I
am going to my Father's; and though with great difficulty I
am got hither, yet now I do not repent me of all the trouble
I have been at to arrive where I am. My sword I give to him
that shall succeed me in my pilgrimage, and my courage and
skill to him that can get it. My marks and scars I carry with
me, to be a witness for me that I have fought His battles who
now will be my rewarder. When the day that he must go hence
was come, many accompanied him to the river side, into which
as he went he said, Death, where is thy sting? And as he went
down deeper, he said, Grave, where is thy victory? So he
passed over, and all the trumpets sounded for him on the
other side.

— John Bunyan.

THE NEW EDITION

You see I have some reason to wish that, in a future state, I may not only be as well as I was, but a little better. And I hope it; for I trust in God. And when I observe that there is great frugality, as well as wisdom in his works, since he has been evidently sparing both of labor and materials; for by the various wonderful inventions of propagation he has provided for the continual peopling of his world with plants and animals, without being at the trouble of repeated new creations; and by the natural reduction of compound substances to their original elements, capable of being employed in new compositions, he has prevented the necessity of creating new matter, so that the earth, water, air, and perhaps fire, which, being compounded from wood, do, when the wood is dissolved, return and again become air, earth, fire, and water; I say that when I see nothing annihilated, and not even a drop of water wasted, I cannot suspect the annihilation of souls, or believe that he will suffer the daily waste of millions of minds ready made that now exist and put himself to the continual trouble of making new ones. Thus, finding myself to exist in the world, I believe I shall, in some shape or other, always exist; and, with all the inconveniences human life is liable to, I shall not object to a new edition of mine; hoping, however, that the errata of the last may be corrected.

— *Benjamin Franklin.*

ROBIN ELLIOTT

What happened was this — on December 22, Robin rode out on his bicycle — to buy us Christmas presents — and at Banbury Cross came into full collision with a big lorry. He could have known nothing more than a momentary impression and surprise, and died shortly after he was taken to the hospital.

As a tiny one at home, he knew the old rhyme — " Ride a Cock Horse to Banbury Cross." Neither he nor we could know then that in after years he himself would come riding to Banbury Cross, and that there he would meet in a flash of sudden glory a whole host of " shining ones " gathered together to greet him. That is what really happened.

We do not think of our Robin as dead — he who was always so much alive. He is not dead. He is much more alive than we are, his eyes on far horizons that we cannot see, his warm young heart aglow with love and hope, his whole eager nature intent already on the thrilling work that God is giving him to do.

He is not asleep, as some may think. What we have laid reverently away was his overcoat, as we describe it to his little brother Michael. He himself in his shining uniform — too full of light for eyes like ours to see it — has gone on.

Yet he has not gone from us. How we miss him in his coming and going no words can tell. But we know that he does come and go — more than ever; that he is with us round the fire in a home circle still unbroken. But for his great shining we should see him. Nevertheless in his own way he will make himself known and speak to us of his life and our life — more deeply shared than ever before — and of what the Wise Ones say.

We do not believe that God called him — even for some higher service. What we do believe is that, when a thing like this happens, God can take it and weave it so gloriously into the pattern of our lives that one day we shall shout when we behold it — for wonder and for joy. It is for us to see to it, as Robin will most surely see to it, that, in quiet faith and humility of heart and surrender of our wills to the Great Loving Will, we help and never hinder the hand of God which is at work upon us.

Being then so very confident of all this — that there is no death here, nor separation, nor loss — we do not feel that Robin's young life has been cut off in the fresh spring blossom of its promise. There is no " might have been " for him. If he might have been a great artist, as we think — for he drew and painted wonderfully — he will still be that. He will roam across wide landscapes, unknown as yet to any of us, where colors change and blend as no mortal eye can see them and sing themselves into music as they shine. There shall he " draw the thing as he sees it for the God of things as they are."

If, as both his schools had hoped, he might have been a leader of men, he still shall lead, and find the way for us and them the more easily from that high plane of his life. And in all that he was and is — his deep love for us, his strong sense of justice and fair play, his great compassion for suffering folk (including tiny animals), his will at every turn to be unselfish and to do his duty — he goes from strength to strength. For his young untiring energies and for his eager burning spirit he shall find wondrous scope both here on earth and in those wider ranges of the soul that we call heaven.

So we think of our very dear Robin. Help us to think that always. Our only picture of him is of a happy-hearted, laughing boy. That is what he was and still is. We shall never say, " How Robin would have laughed! " but, as we have said already, " How Robin must be laughing! " For he is not a proud and happy memory. He is a radiant, living, loving person, round about us. We know it.

That is our faith. So help us, God.

— *Canon W. H. Elliott.*

They Live

Tell me, tell yourselves fairly, is your flesh, your body, the part of yourself which you can see and handle, YOU? You know that it is not. When a neighbor's body dies, you say, perhaps, "He is dead," but you say it carelessly; and when one whom you know well, and love, dies — when a parent, a wife, a child, dies — you feel very differently about him, even if you do not speak differently. You feel and know that he, the person whom you loved and understood, and felt with, and felt for, here on earth, is not dead at all; you feel (and in proportion as the friend you have lost was loving, and good, and full of feeling for you, you feel it all the more strongly) that your friend, or your child, or the wife of your bosom, is alive still — where you know not, but you feel that they are alive; that they are very near you; that they are thinking of you, watching you, caring for you, perhaps grieving over you when you go wrong, perhaps rejoicing over you when you go right, perhaps helping you, though you cannot see them, in some wonderful way. You know that only their mortal flesh is dead, that their mortal flesh was all you put into the grave; but that they themselves, their souls and spirits, which were their very and real selves, are alive forevermore; and you trust and hope to meet them when you die; ay, to meet them body and soul too, at the last day, the very same persons whom you knew here on earth, though the flesh which they wore here in this life has crumbled into dust years and ages before.

Is not this true? Is not this a blessed life-giving thought — I had almost said the most blessed and life-giving thought man can have — that those whom we have loved and lost are not dead, but only gone before; that they live still to God and with God; that only their flesh has perished, and they themselves are alive forevermore?

— *Charles Kingsley, in* Sermons for the Times.

O Time and Change! — with hair as gray
As was my sire's that winter day,
How strange it seems, with so much gone
Of life and love, to still live on!
Ah, brother! only I and thou
Are left of all that circle now, —
The dear home faces whereupon
That fitful firelight paled and shone.
Henceforward, listen as we will,
The voices of that hearth are still;
Look where we may, the wide earth o'er,
Those lighted faces smile no more.
We tread the paths their feet have worn,
　　We sit beneath their orchard-trees,
　　We hear, like them, the hum of bees
And rustle of the bladed corn;
We turn the pages that they read,
　　Their written words we linger o'er,
But in the sun they cast no shade,
No voice is heard, no sign is made,
　　No step is on the conscious floor!
Yet love will dream, and faith will trust
(Since He who knows our need is just)
That somehow, somewhere, meet we must.
Alas for him who never sees
The stars shine through his cypress-trees!
Who, hopeless, lays his dead away,
Nor looks to see the breaking day
Across the mournful marbles play!
Who hath not learned, in hours of faith,
　　The truth to flesh and sense unknown,
That Life is ever lord of Death,
　　And Love can never lose its own!
　　　　　　　　　— *John Greenleaf Whittier.*